Nanas Around the World

A Universal Tribute of Love to Our Grandchildren

Written by Margaret Long
Illustrated by Phil Thys

Family Tree Publishing

Nanas Around the World ©2020 by Margaret Long
All rights reserved.

LEGAL DISCLAIMER: No part of this book may be reproduced or transmitted in any form or by any means, electronic or mechanical, including photocopying, recording or by any information storage and retrieval system, without written permission from the author. You may not reprint, resell or distribute the contents of this book without express written permission from the author.

All violations will be remedied with legal action and justice will be sought to the maximum penalty allowable by law in the State in which the original purchaser resides.

Illustrations: Phil Thys

Managing Editor: Robin Shukle
Design and Production: Liz Mrofka

Family Tree Publishing
Fort Collins, Colorado

Printed by Kindle Direct Publishing

ISBN-13: 979-8569138166

Dedication

To all Nanas, Grandmas, and Omas of every culture who proudly serve in the "*Grandparent Honor Guard*", my term that describes the honor we feel, the strong bond we hold in sharing our unique, universal, and boundless love for our grandchildren.

To my brother, Phil who interpreted my words and emotions as a new grandparent, then so beautifully and artistically captured the true essence of our cultural similarities. For this I am extremely grateful.

To my mom, our family's beloved "Nana Joan".
Your love lives on within your seven kids,
thirteen grandkids, and six great grandkids . . . and counting!

To my mother in law, Marjorie, our family's "Grandma Long".
Your unique and playful relationship with each grandchild
and great grandchild is greatly cherished.

Thank you, and God Bless.
Nana M.

News of your expected arrival
kissed my heart,
a precious new life beginning
its glorious start!

God sent His guardian angel
to kiss your soul,
oh, how I will cherish my new
grandparent role!

Daily prayers were said until
we finally met,
a wondrous day which I will
never forget!

My heart so full of love and the grandest of wishes,
my way to show you will be through Nana Kisses!

A blanket of love to cover
lands far and wide,
in the hearts of Nanas around
the world, your gift will reside.

When you are small and as
you continue to grow,
Nana kisses brings to you a love
that you will always know!

Your presence to me is a blessing
and a pleasure,
Nana kisses are your key to the
most special treasure!

In the evening as you lay
your head down good night,
Nana kisses bring you sweet dreams
until the morning light!

Then as you rise for a brand-new day, you will know the sun and my kisses are here to stay!

It could be a kiss good bye or a kiss hello, but with you, Nana kisses will always go!

Gentle hands blending love and
guidance that will help shape your soul,
Nana kisses are comforting treats
like the dough found in the bottom
of the bowl!

We celebrate your successes
with great pride and cheers,
Nana kisses will follow you
throughout your many years!

An abundant of kisses are
sure to mount,
at least 1,000 a day by
this Nana's count!

2 6 17 11 100 8 473 19 9
36 20 96 13 36 19 5 32
798 4 87 14 27
21 12 23 45 325
400 761 18 64 22 30 145
117 92 300 35 1 700 90 27
16 50 29 922 88 95 333
33 67 25 34 279 111 62
25 60 3 45 39
821 78 50
7 28 999 365 99 68 47 200 777 88
42 10 31 15 24
59 26 78 1000 91 48 93 62

I pledge my love through every season,
Nana kisses can be for
ANY reason!

So whether you are here,
there, near or far,
Nana Kisses will reach
you wherever you are!

Made in the USA
Columbia, SC
22 December 2020